Energy

Andrew Charman

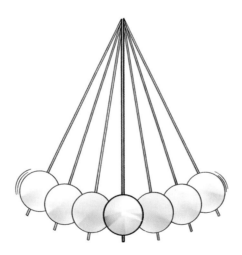

FRANKLIN WATTS

New York/London/Toronto/Sydney

© Franklin Watts 1992

Franklin Watts, Inc
95 Madison Avenue
New York, NY 10016

Library of Congress Cataloging-in-Publication Data

Charman, Andrew.
    Energy / by Andrew Charman.
        p.   cm. — (Science through art)
    Includes index.
    Summary: Explores how basic principles of energy can be used in
art.
    ISBN 0-531-14233-7
    1. Force and energy—Juvenile literature. 2. Art and science—
—Juvenile literature. 3. Creation (Literary, artistic, etc.)—
—Juvenile literature. [1. Force and energy—Experiments.
2. Experiments. 3. Art and science.] I. Title. II. Series.
Science through art.
QC73.4.C48   1993   92-6079
531'.6—dc20   CIP AC

10 9 8 7 6 5 4 3 2 1

Series Editor: Hazel Poole
Edited by: Cleeve Publishing Services Limited
Design: Edward Kinsey
Artwork: Aziz Khan
Photography: Chris Fairclough
Consultant: Margaret Whalley

Typeset by Lineage, Watford

Printed in the United Kingdom

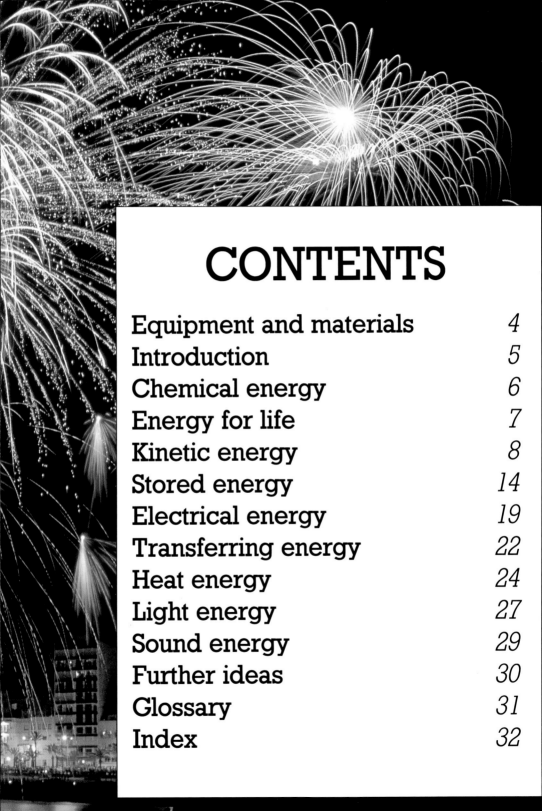

CONTENTS

EQUIPMENT AND MATERIALS

This book describes activities which use the following:

Adhesive (UHU)
Adhesive tape
Batteries (1.5 volt)
Battery holder
Bottles – clear, colorless, and plastic
    – milk bottles (or similar)
Bradawl
Bulb (3.5 volt)
Bulb holder
Candles (small)
Cardboard – thick and oak tag
Compass
Corks (from bottles)
Craft knife
Cutting board
Cutting mat
Electric motor (3 volt)
Fabric
Felt-tip pens
Food colorings
Fruit
Funnel
Fun Tak
Hole punch
Kitchen knife
Marker pen
Measuring cup
Modeling clay
Paintbrush

Paints (gouache)
Paper – plain drawing paper
    – tissue paper
    – tissues
Paper fasteners
Pencil
Plastic (thin and flat, from a margarine container)
Plate (large)
Pliers
Rubber bands
Rulers – metal ruler, for use with the craft knife
    – plastic
Scissors
Screwdriver
Screws
Shoe box
Skewers (wooden and metal)
String
Switch (electrical)
Tape
Thread (cotton)
Tubes (cardboard, various sizes, some with metal bottoms)
Water
Wheel (small)
Wire – florist's wire
    – thin electrical wire
Wood (various sizes)
Yogurt cups

INTRODUCTION

Few things can happen without energy. Your body cannot do anything without energy, whether you are playing, working, or sleeping. A machine cannot do anything without energy, whether it is turning, lifting, bending, pulling, or pushing. A light bulb cannot give light without energy, and without energy a fire cannot give out heat.

Energy is never lost. It can be passed on from one moving part to another and changed from one kind into another. A light bulb turns electrical energy into light and heat energy. A car's engine turns the chemical energy from its fuel into moving, or kinetic, energy. Some energy is also given off as heat and sound. In both cases, the energy is not lost, just changed.

Nearly all the energy on Earth comes first from the sun. Changes and transfers take place to give us the forms of energy we know and use. Sometimes there is a long and complicated series of changes, at other times the chain is simpler. A simple energy chain might start with the sun and end with a girl running. The sun produces light and heat energy. Green plants turn this into chemical energy. The girl eats a plant and turns the chemical energy into kinetic, or moving, energy.

Human beings have developed many complicated ways of gathering and using the sun's energy. In recent years, many people have been trying to find new ways of using energy which are clean and safe, and which produce as little waste as possible.

As you read this book and follow the activities, you will be exploring and discovering the different kinds of energy as a scientist. Like a scientist you will need to question what you are doing, keep records of what happens, and test things to see if you can make them work in different or better ways. By following the activities, you will also be an artist because you will be using the different kinds of energy to make art. The simplest way of using energy to make art is to push and pull a paintbrush across a piece of paper to paint a picture. But art can also be made from things that spin or fall, from light, sound, and heat.

CHEMICAL ENERGY

Energy comes to us from the sun in the form of light and heat. Plants grow by using this energy to combine water from the soil with a gas called carbon dioxide from the air. This happens in the leaves. Green plants change the light energy from the sun into chemical energy. They cannot grow without light.

Stand under a tree in summer and look up through the leaves to the sky. You cannot see much of the sky, because the sun is helping the leaves to grow.

Plants take light energy from the sun and turn it into chemical energy which is stored in their leaves, stems, and roots.

Some kinds of hedges can be cut into interesting shapes. This is called topiary. It is a kind of art which uses living plants.

Plants come in many shapes, and sizes, often with bright, colorful flowers. Gardeners plan their gardens to make the most of this variety. This is also a kind of art.

Human beings and animals need energy for everything they do. We get our energy by eating food. We take the chemical energy from the food and turn it into kinetic energy, or energy of motion, to fuel the muscles in our bodies. This food can be plants, or animals that have already eaten plants. When we make a fancy meal and arrange the food in a way that is interesting or fun to look at, you could say that we are making art.

Can you think of other ways in which we can make food look good? You can find lots of examples by looking through cookbooks, in magazines, or in store windows.

People enjoy making food that looks attractive or fun. This is food art.

Food Art

You will need: a cutting board, a kitchen knife, different kinds of fruit, a plate, and wooden skewers.

1. Gather together a number of different kinds of fruit. Look at them closely to see what kinds of shapes they will make when sliced.

2. Slice up some of the fruit and make a collage with the slices. You can also use the pits and skin. Eat the fruit afterward. Never waste food – wasted food is wasted energy.

3. Try making a sculpture with whole fruit. You can join the fruit together with the skewers. Eat the fruit while it is still fresh.

KINETIC ENERGY

Any object that moves has kinetic, or moving, energy. Your arm as it swings has kinetic energy; so does a ball as it rolls, or water as it tumbles down a waterfall or flows along a stream. The wind has kinetic energy which is passed on to the blades of a windmill. Many artists make objects that are designed to move. This is called kinetic art. You can also make kinetic art with something that moves, even though the finished object is supposed to stand still.

Think of a typical day in your life. Try to remember all the ways in which you use kinetic energy.
  Wind has lots of kinetic energy. Think of some ways it was once used and how it is used today. There are forms of transportation that use the energy of the wind – see if you can name them.

The kinetic energy of the wind is passed on to the blades of a wind turbine. The kinetic energy can then be used to make electrical energy.

When you roll a ball, you use the chemical energy that is stored in your body to give your arm kinetic energy. This energy is then passed on to the ball.

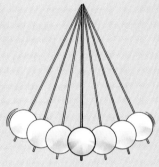

A pendulum has kinetic energy as it swings.

Paint pendulum

You will need: an empty yogurt cup, a metal skewer, string, paint, newspaper, plain paper, Fun Tak, scissors, and water.
1. With the skewer, make two holes opposite each other in the top of the pot. Make another hole in the bottom of the pot.

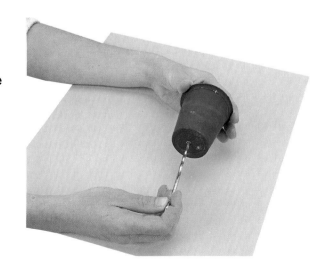

2. Tie a short length of string between the two holes. Attach a longer piece of string to the short piece so that the cup hangs like a pendulum.

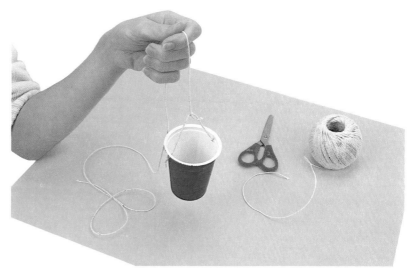

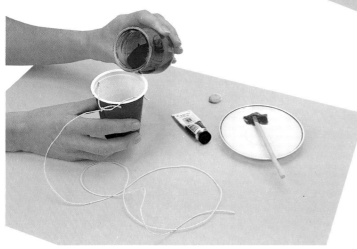

3. Cover the hole in the bottom of the cup, on the outside, with Fun Tak. Fill the cup about one quarter full with runny paint.

4. Cover a large area with newspaper and place a sheet of plain paper in the middle. Hang the cup so that it swings about 2 inches above the paper. Remove the Fun Tak and swing the cup.

5. Pendulum art!

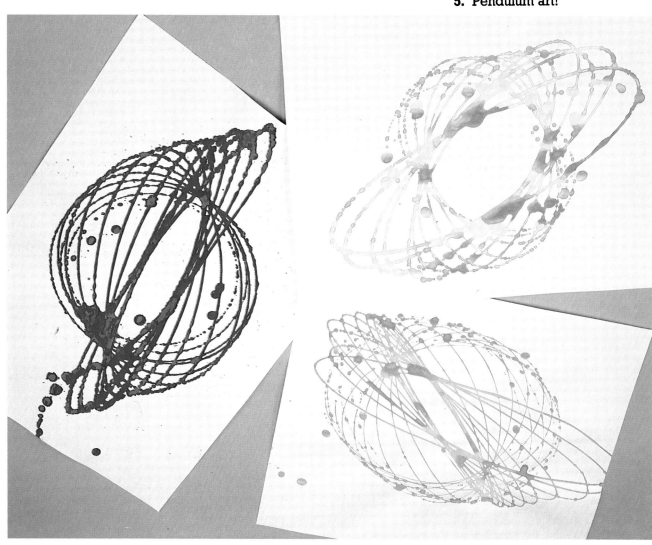

Wind-powered dancer

You will need: a cardboard tube, a length of thick wire, scissors, a paper fastener, felt-tip pens, a compass, cardboard, a ruler, a pencil, and a craft knife.

1. Draw and cut three circles from the cardboard. They need to be slightly smaller in diameter than the tube. Fold two of these circles in half.

2. Stick the folded circles to the flat circle to form a four-bladed turbine. With tape, stick the wire to the turbine so that the wire becomes an axle.

3. Paint the tube. Cut two notches opposite each other in one end of the tube. Push the paper fastener into one of the notches from the outside and make it secure.

4. Put the turbine into the tube. One end of the axle should sit inside the head of the paper fastener. You may need to cut a length off the axle.

5. Draw and cut out a figure that will turn on the axle. Color it in.

6. Tape the figure to the upright axle. When you blow into the tube, the kinetic energy of your breath will turn the turbine and give the figure kinetic energy, too.

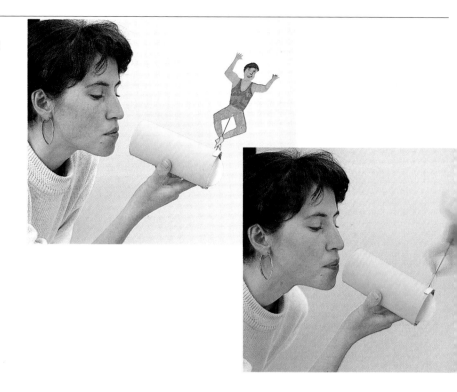

Kinetic puppet

You will need: string, scissors, cardboard, a pencil, paints, a brush, water, wire, tape, a wide cardboard tube 6 inches long, paper fasteners, a metal skewer, a hole punch, and wire cutters.

1. Draw on the cardboard and then cut out: a circle about 4 inches across, a strip 5 inches × ¾ inch, and a cardboard puppet with separate head, arms, and legs. Punch holes where the puppet will be jointed.

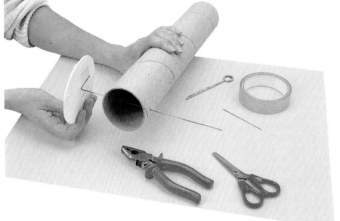

2. Make a hole near the outside edge of the circle. Attach a length of wire to the cardboard circle. Push the other end through the top of the cardboard tube.

3. Make a hole at each end of the cardboard strip. Attach a piece of wire to the middle of the strip and push this through the tube below the circle, as shown.

4. Paint the puppet and, when dry, join together the legs, arms, head, and body with the paper fasteners. The limbs should move freely. Attach the puppet to the tube below the cardboard strip with a fastener.

5. Attach a length of string from the circle to the strip. Also tie lengths of string from the arms to the strip and from the arms to the legs.

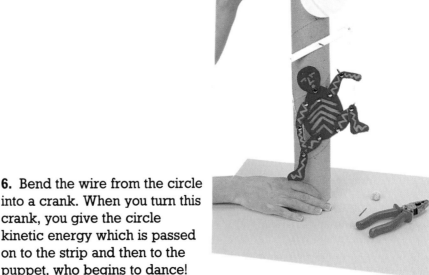

6. Bend the wire from the circle into a crank. When you turn this crank, you give the circle kinetic energy which is passed on to the strip and then to the puppet, who begins to dance!

STORED ENERGY

Stored energy is energy that is not doing anything, but is ready to be released. There are many different ways of storing energy and these stores can be released to make most forms of energy, including kinetic, light, sound, and heat.

Look around your house. See how many things in it use or can use batteries. Think of some reasons why batteries are sometimes more useful than mains electricity.

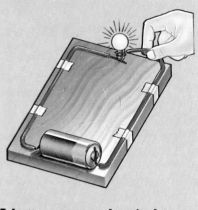

Any object raised above the ground has a kind of energy stored called gravitational potential energy. This is because the force called gravity is ready to bring it back to the ground when it is released.

A battery stores chemical energy. When it is connected to a circuit, it releases this store as electrical energy.

Creature on a spring

You will need: a length of wire, a plastic marker pen, a cork, oak tag or paper, felt-tip pens, tissue paper, scissors, and glue.
1. Wind the wire around the plastic pen to make a spring. Leave ¾ inch of straight wire at one end. Push this straight end into the cork.

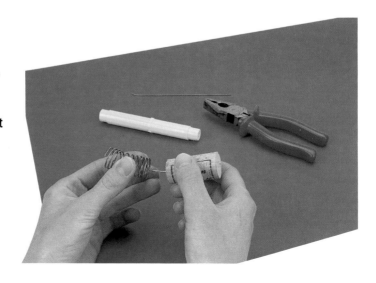

2. Draw a face onto the oak tag or paper and glue it to the cork. Draw and cut some tail feathers from the tissue paper and glue them on too.

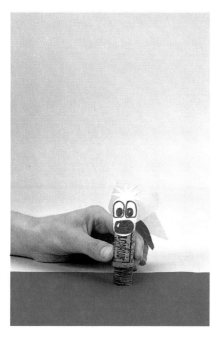

3. Hold the cork between your finger and thumb and push down onto a firm surface to squeeze the spring.

4. Let go of the cork and the spring creature will leap into the air.

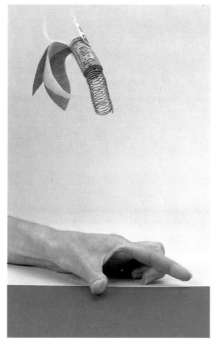

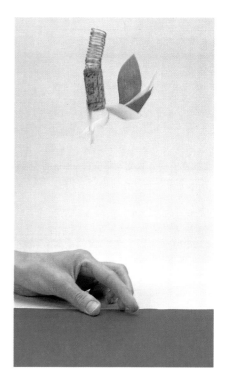

Water-powered picture

You will need: a clear, colorless plastic bottle, a cork, a plastic lid (from a margarine tub), two wooden skewers, a measuring cup, a funnel, scissors, a craft knife, a metal skewer, Fun Tak, cardboard, felt-tip pens, and a craft knife.

1. Cut the bottom off the plastic bottle. Decide where your "turbine" is going to be and make two holes opposite each other for the axles.

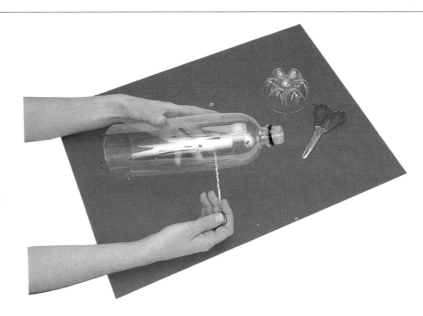

2. Cut out four rectangles of flat plastic. These will be the blades of the turbine. Make four equally spaced cuts in the cork and slide the plastic rectangles into these cuts.

3. Hold the turbine inside the bottle and push the wooden skewers through holes from the outside into the cork. The skewers are the axles.

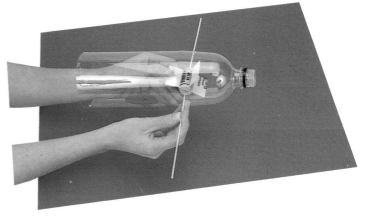

4. Stand the bottle in a large margarine tub. Hold the cardboard up against the bottle and mark the position of the axle. Make a hole in the cardboard for the axle to go through.

5. On the cardboard, draw a picture which includes a moving part. Draw and cut out the moving part separately.

6. Prop up the picture against the bottle. Make it secure with tape or Fun Tak. Push the axle through the hole and attach the moving part to it. You may need to trim the axle first.

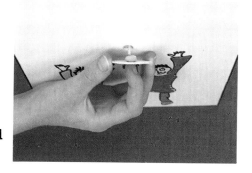

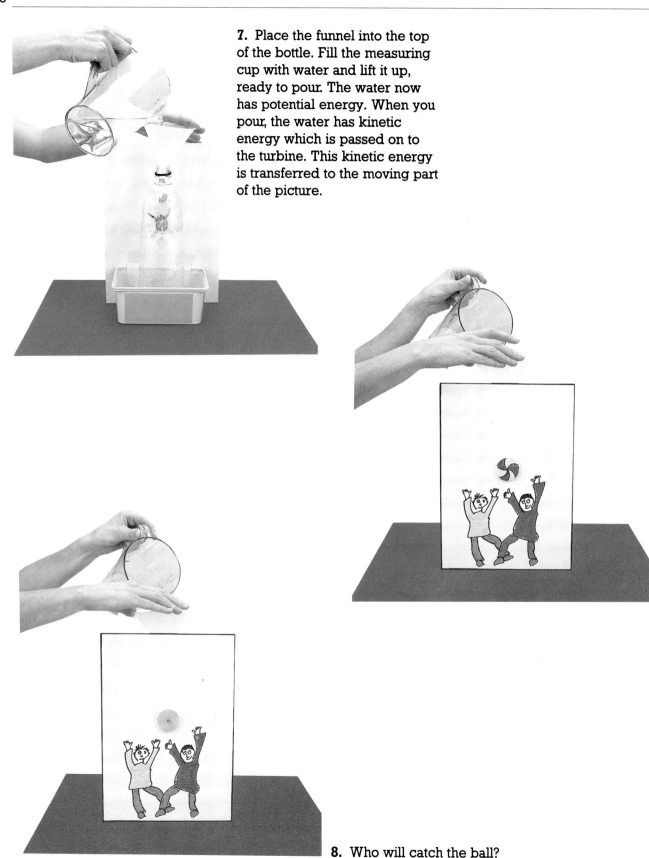

7. Place the funnel into the top of the bottle. Fill the measuring cup with water and lift it up, ready to pour. The water now has potential energy. When you pour, the water has kinetic energy which is passed on to the turbine. This kinetic energy is transferred to the moving part of the picture.

8. Who will catch the ball?

ELECTRICAL ENERGY

Electrical energy is used to provide light and heat in homes, to drive motors in trains, cars, and toys, and to make radios and televisions work. The energy to do these things comes from the energy in the electric current.

Every substance is made of atoms. Each atom has a nucleus and electrons that travel around it. An electric current is produced when electrons jump from one atom to the next.

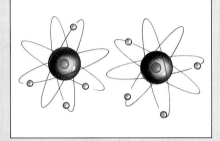

There are many changes of energy which happen so that you can turn on a switch and get light energy out of a bulb. The energy chain starts with the sun.

Light from the sun makes trees grow (light energy to chemical energy).

The coal is mined and taken to a power plant where it is burned (chemical to heat energy).

Over millions of years the trees have become coal (chemical energy).

The burning coal heats water to make steam. The steam drives a turbine (heat to kinetic energy).

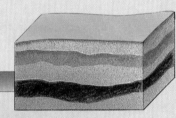

The electric current reaches your house and you turn on the switch. The wire inside the bulb heats up (electrical energy to light and heat energy).

The turbine spins and produces an electric current (kinetic to electrical energy).

How many things do you have that use electrical energy? Think about how you would live without them. How would you make light, or heat?

Many people are trying to find ways of making electrical energy from the wind, the movement of the sea and the sun. These are called "alternative" energy sources. You might like to find out how they work.

Spinning pictures

You will need: a block of wood, a flat piece of wood, tape, an electric motor, thin electrical wire, batteries (1.5 volt) in a battery holder, two paper clips, two alligator clips, Fun Tak, a compass, scissors, cardboard, paints, a paintbrush, water, glue, a small wheel, a screwdriver, and a ruler.

1. Glue the two pieces of wood together so that they make a sturdy base for your spinning pictures.

2. Attach the motor to the block of wood with the tape. The central axle of the motor should be pointing upward and be clear of the wood.

3. Attach alligator clips to the wires and connect the batteries (in their holder) to the motor. Unclip one of the alligator clips to stop the motor from running. Secure the batteries to the wood with Fun Tak.

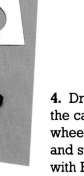

4. Draw and cut out a disk from the cardboard. Attach the small wheel to the shaft of the motor and stick the disk to this wheel with Fun Tak.

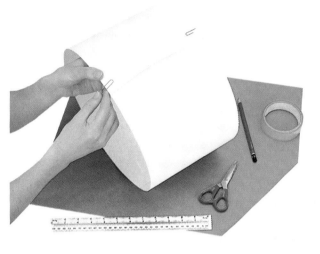

5. Cut a piece of cardboard, twice the height of your block and motor and long enough to encircle them. Join the ends together with paper clips. This will fit over the motor and act as a splash barrier.

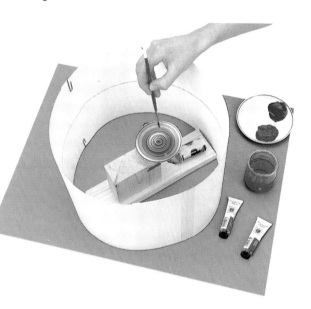

6. Reconnect the batteries to the motor and put the splash barrier in place. Paint the spinning disk by gently touching it with the brush.

7. Electrical energy from the batteries produces kinetic energy in the disk, which you then use to produce your art work.

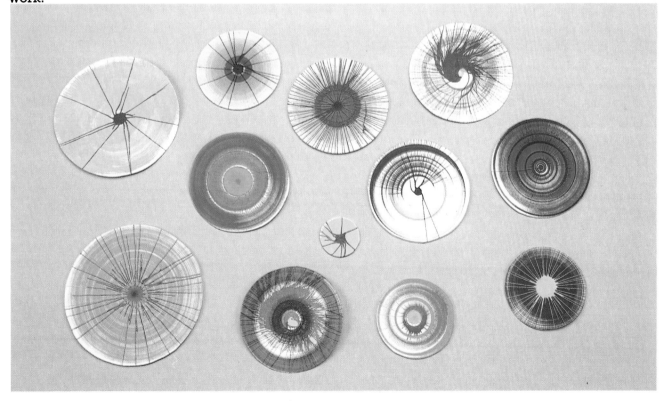

Energy is never lost. It can be changed into another form of energy or it can be transferred or passed on from one moving part to another. Machines do not make more energy than is put into them, they simply transfer the energy from one part to another to make better use of it.

Think of more examples of machines that transfer energy. You may like to visit a factory or look closely at an old steam engine, to see how the energy is transferred from one part to another.

Have a look at a bicycle with gears. Different size gears affect how you pedal. Larger gears make pedaling more difficult than small ones.

The small wheel turns quickly. The energy is transferred by the belt to the big wheel, which turns more slowly. Friction is the force that keeps the belt in place and enables the transfer to happen.

When you pedal a bicycle the kinetic energy of the gear with the pedals is transferred by the chain to the back wheel.

Revolving sea picture

You will need: a piece of wood (approximately 2¾ × ½ × 10 inches), three short screws, three cardboard tubes (with metal bottoms), a bradawl, a screwdriver, paints, a paintbrush, two large rubber bands, glue, and paper.

1. Paint a background scene onto the tubes. You can paint details, such as the fish, on a separate piece of paper.

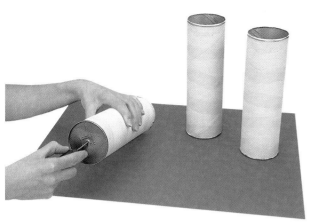

2. With the bradawl, make a hole in the center of the bottom of each tube. Ask an adult to help you with this.

3. Screw the tubes to the wood, but do not tighten the screws – the tubes should turn easily. Position the tubes so that they are close to each other but not touching.

4. Put a rubber band around the first and second tube, and another around the second and third. Glue the fish to the tubes.

5. When you turn the first tube, the energy you pass on to it will be transferred to the other two by the rubber bands.

HEAT ENERGY

Heat is also a kind of energy. It can travel very fast and always moves from a warm place to a cooler one. Heat moves, or transfers its energy, in three different ways. The heat from the sun travels in waves through space. This is called radiation. Heat can also enter and travel through a solid as heat is transferred from one molecule to another. This is called conduction. Heat energy entering a gas or liquid causes convection currents. As the gas or liquid heats up, it expands and becomes less dense. This makes it rise. Cold gas or liquid takes its place.

Make a list of several things that make heat. This heat is useful or "wasted" heat.

Find a radiator that is hot. Notice that it is hotter above the radiator than at its side, because heat rises.

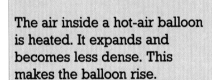

The air inside a hot-air balloon is heated. It expands and becomes less dense. This makes the balloon rise.

The heat energy from the sun can be collected by solar panels. The energy can be used to heat water and make electricity.

Heat mobile

You will need: tin foil pie plate or cupcake cases, a dowel rod, modeling clay, a compass, cotton thread, a length of wire (or coat hanger), saucers, small candles, a block of wood, and some Fun Tak.

1. Mold a large lump of modeling clay to the block of wood and push the dowel rod into it.

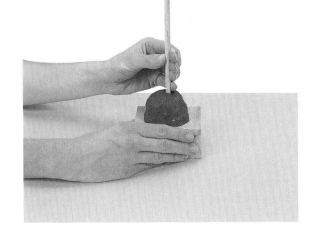

2. Make a kink in each end of the wire and attach it to the top of the dowel rod with Fun Tak.

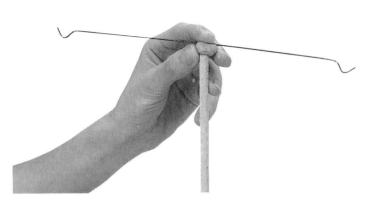

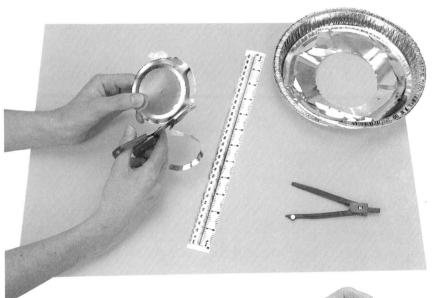

3. Cut a circle from the foil dish, about 3 inches across. Cut this circle into a spiral.

4. Carefully make a hole in the middle of the spiral with the point of a compass. Pull a length of thread through the hole and attach it to one end of the wire crosspiece.

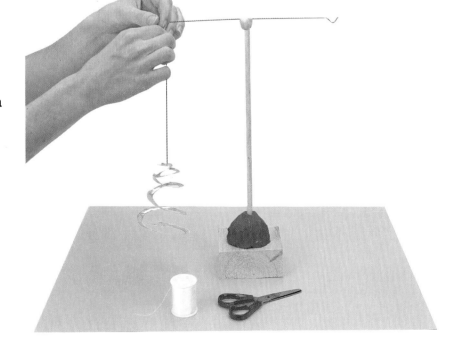

5. Ask an adult to light the candle and place it under the spiral. The warm air rising from the flame will make the spiral spin.

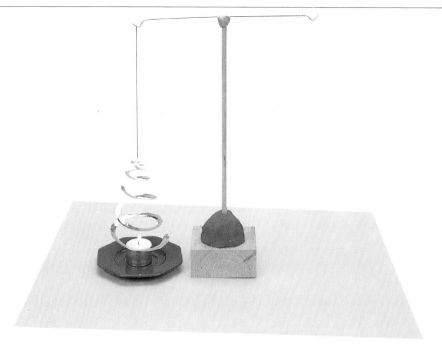

6. Try other foil designs to see if they will spin.

WARNING: NEVER LEAVE A CANDLE BURNING WHEN YOU LEAVE A ROOM. DO NOT PUT THE MOBILE NEAR ANYTHING THAT WILL BURN EASILY.

Light energy travels in waves. The light from the sun travels at 985 million feet per second and takes about eight minutes to reach us. Most of the light we see comes from hot objects. The hotter an object becomes the closer it gets to giving off white light. The pure white light we get from the sun is produced by temperatures of about 10,830°F.

See how many different sources of light you can find. Look around at home, at school, in stores, or in a car.

Lights are not only used to help us see in the dark. Think of what else they are used for.

A tungsten bulb gives off light energy because the wire inside it gets very hot. In this situation, the heat is wasted energy.

Magic lantern

You will need: an empty shoe box, glue, cardboard, a pencil, a ruler, scissors, a craft knife, colored tissue paper, batteries, and a battery holder, thin electrical wire, a switch, a bulb, and a bulb holder.

1. Cut a small hole in one end of the shoe box. Cut four rectangles of cardboard that are as long as the box is high and 1 inch wide. Score and fold these lengthwise.

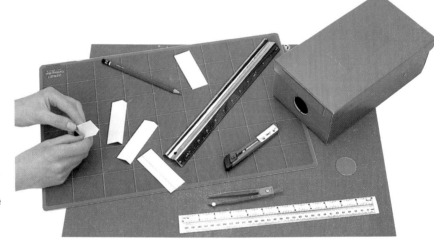

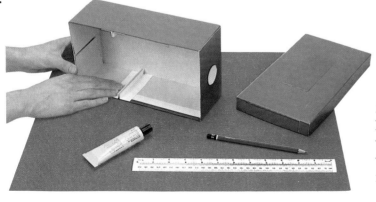

2. Glue the rectangles into the box about two-thirds of the way up the box from the hole. Glue them so that they make a slot ⅛ inch wide.

3. From the cardboard cut two frames that are the same width and height as the box. Glue tissue paper onto one of these to make a picture. Place the second frame over the first to "enclose" the picture.

4. Connect the batteries to the switch and the bulb as shown.

5. Mount the batteries and bulb onto cardboard and then glue them as a block into the end section of the box. Slip the picture into the slots and flick the switch so that the bulb lights up.

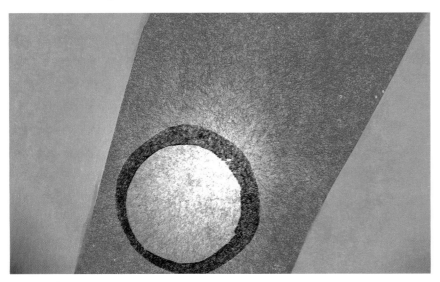

6. Put the lid back on the box. You can now see your "slide" through the hole. It is lit up by light energy from the bulb.

SOUND ENERGY

When something has kinetic energy it usually produces waste sound energy, too. This is why machines are often noisy. When a falling object hits the ground, unless it bounces, its kinetic energy is changed into other forms of energy. Some of the energy goes to change the shape of the object, some is lost as heat, and some of it is changed into sound energy.

> Make a list of different kinds of musical instruments. Put them into groups according to how the sound is made.
>   Find an empty can and hit it. Fill it with something and then hit it again. The can will make a different sound.

When you hit a drum, the kinetic energy of the moving drumstick is transferred to the skin of the drum, which vibrates. This vibration makes sound waves.

Inside a clarinet is a reed. The air from your lungs has kinetic energy and this is transferred to the reed, causing it to vibrate. It is the vibration that makes the sound.

Compose your own music.

You will need: three empty bottles of the same size, food colorings, water, a dowel rod, two yogurt cups, glue, rice, some material, and two rubber bands.

1. Fill the bottles with different amounts of water and color the water with drops of food coloring.

2. Blow across the open neck of each bottle or hit them with the dowel rod. Changing the amount of water changes the sound.

3. Glue the yogurt cups together. Put rice in each cup and cover the open end with a piece of fabric. Secure with a rubber band. You now have a shaker.

Magic lantern slides

You can build up a collection of slides to use with your magic lantern. They can be patterns or pictures of things. You can draw or paint onto tissue paper to create a different effect.

Energy collage

There are many different forms of energy and human beings have developed lots of ways of collecting and transferring them. Make a collage picture on the theme of energy.

Kinetic energy pictures

There are lots of ways we can harness the energy of falling water to make art in the way that we did on page 18. Make some more pictures with moving parts.

A photographic study

Use a camera to take photographs of how we use energy. You can begin with some of the ideas mentioned in this book.

GLOSSARY

Atom
Everything, including chemicals, is made up of tiny particles called atoms. A tiny speck of dust contains about 1000 billion atoms.

Battery
A battery is made up of a number of electrical cells joined together. The cells produce electricity. Batteries are used to power many things including flashlights, radios, and cars.

Chemical energy
Every substance on Earth is made of atoms grouped together to form chemicals. This includes our food. The chemicals we eat are broken down inside our bodies to release energy.

Circuit
An electrical circuit is usually a loop of wire along which electricity flows. A bulb put into this circuit will light up.

Current
An electrical current is a flow of electrical charge. This charge is caused by electrons jumping from one atom in a substance to the next.

Density
The density of a substance is the amount of mass or material that it has for every unit of its volume. A lump of rock has more mass than water of the same volume. This makes it denser, and it sinks.

Electrons
Electrons are contained within an atom and spin around its nucleus, making many billions of trips in a second.

Fahrenheit
A scale for measuring temperature. Freezing point is 32° Fahrenheit, 212° Fahrenheit is boiling point. This scale is also known as the Fahrenheit scale.

Force
A force changes the shape or motion of an object by pushing, pulling, stretching, or squeezing it.

Fuel
A material from which energy is released. Oil and coal are fuels that release their energy when they are burned. Food is fuel for bodies.

Gas
The particles that make up a gas are more loosely held together than they are in a solid or a liquid. This makes the gas move freely to fill whatever space is available. The air we breathe contains many gases.

Gravity
The force of attraction between matter. Gravity is what keeps things on the earth and what keeps the planets orbiting around the sun.

Kinetic energy
A moving object or substance has kinetic energy. The wind, falling water, a rolling ball, and a flying airplane all have kinetic energy.

Machine
A simple machine is used to help people do things. A lever is an example of a simple machine.

Nucleus
An atomic nucleus is the inner part of an atom.

Pendulum
A weight hanging from a fixed point. It swings back and forth at a regular rate.

Potential energy
A kind of stored energy. Any object lifted above the ground has potential energy because the force of gravity will eventually bring it down again. Water has potential energy when it is stored in a tank in your attic.

Solar energy
Energy from the sun. It comes to us in the form of light and heat energy.

Solid
A material in which the atoms are held firmly together. A solid is rigid and holds its shape, unlike a gas or a liquid.

Spring
A length of wire wound into a coil. It can be squeezed or stretched.

Turbine
A device for turning the motion of wind or water into kinetic energy. It usually has blades turned at an angle so that the wind or water pushes against them.

Vibration
Moving backward and forward very quickly.

Additional photographs: Zefa 2-3, 5.